S0-EGI-644

# Family Farm

Written by: Susan Clewis

Ilustrated by: Laura Gessford

## This book belongs to:

Name: _____

## Book 66 - Concept: aw/au

**Red Words:** a, again, are, as, come, could, do, four, from, good, has, have, into, is, put, the, there, they, to, took, tractor, use(ed), was, where, work, would

**Vocabulary:** bales, bedding, hay, peach, plum, straw, tend

**Word Count:** 303

Farmily Farm (Book 66)
Set C Decodable Reader (2nd Edition)
Written by: Susan Clewis
Edited by: Amy Gulley
Illustrated by: Laura Gessford

ISBN: 978-1-948926-43-0

imse.com

My name is Paul. I am from a tiny town. My gramps and gram have a farm not far away. I like to go see my gramps and gram.

My Uncle Saul helps on the farm. They work on the farm from sunup to sundown. There are cows to feed, gardens to tend, and grass to cut. There are trees with peaches and plums that we sell at the roadside stand. In the spring, I help gather and put them in baskets to sell.

Fresh Peaches and Plums

My gramps plants hay and straw for the cows. The straw is used for bedding in the barn. The hay is used to feed the cows. Gramps has a big tractor that is used to put the hay into bales.

The best thing to do when I go to the farm is to ride around on the four-wheeler with Uncle Saul. One day my uncle and I saw tree branches on the ground that needed to be cleaned up. It was an awful mess! I helped get the branches off the ground, and my uncle used a chainsaw to cut them into little logs. The sawdust made me sneeze!

Uncle Saul and I hauled the logs to the trailer, which was connected to the four-wheeler. We took the logs to the barn, where they could be stored until winter. We knew they would be needed to help heat the home when it turned colder. The hard work made me sleepy, and I yawned as we drove away from the barn.

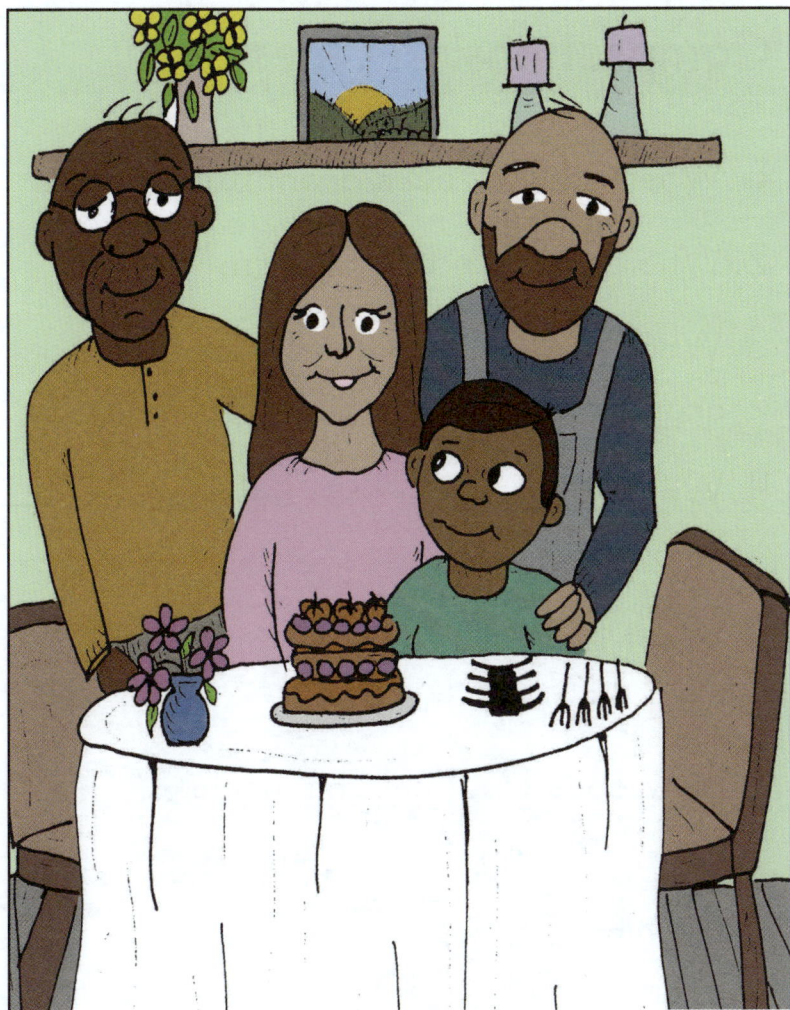

At the end of the day, my gram had dinner waiting for us. She had made a peach shortcake as a treat. The cake was complete with whipped cream! It was so good that I asked her to make it again when I come back in August!

# Comprehension Questions

1. Where does Paul's grandfather live?

2. Who helps him on the farm?

3. What are some of the things his grandfather grows on the farm?

4. What is the difference between straw and hay?

5. What is Paul's favorite thing to do when he visits the farm?

6. How does Paul help his uncle?

7. What does Paul's grandmother make for him?

## Writing Activity

Have you ever been on a farm? What did you see? If you've never been on a farm, what do you think it would be like? Write about it.